AF442382

THEORY AND PRACTICAL OF EVERY ACTION

(BASED ON BHAGAVAD GITA CHAPTER-5)

DR. JAGADEESH PILLAI

Copyright © Dr. Jagadeesh Pillai
All Rights Reserved.

This book has been published with all efforts taken to make the material error-free after the consent of the author. However, the author and the publisher do not assume and hereby disclaim any liability to any party for any loss, damage, or disruption caused by errors or omissions, whether such errors or omissions result from negligence, accident, or any other cause.

While every effort has been made to avoid any mistake or omission, this publication is being sold on the condition and understanding that neither the author nor the publishers or printers would be liable in any manner to any person by reason of any mistake or omission in this publication or for any action taken or omitted to be taken or advice rendered or accepted on the basis of this work. For any defect in printing or binding the publishers will be liable only to replace the defective copy by another copy of this work then available.

Contents

Prayer   *vii*

Dedicated To   *ix*

About The Author   *xi*

Preface   *xvii*

THEORY AND PRACTICAL OF EVERY ACTION

English Text Of Sanskrit Slokhas Of Chapter-5 For Quick Reference

Contact   53

Prayer

HARE RAMA HARE RAMA, RAMA RAMA HARE HARE
- HARE KRISHNA, HARE KRISHNA, KRISHNA
KRISHNA, HARE HARE

(Mantra - Kali Santaranopanishad)

Dedicated To

|| ALL THOSE IN THE SPIRITUAL PATH TO ATTAIN
WISDOM AND KNOWLEDGE TO REMOVE
IGNORANCE ||

About The Author

Dr. Jagadeesh Pillai a voracious reader, Four Times Guinness World Record holder, writer, and true research scholar was born in Varanasi, the abode of Lord Shiva. He is Ph.D. in Vedic Science. He is a multi-faceted polymath with innate qualities, creative ideas and many remarkable achievements. Although his roots extend back to "Gods own Country"(Kerala), the residents of Varanasi feel proud of him and adore him as a child of Varanasi who caters to every individual in need without any expectations. A deep study into his profile reflects that he has added so many feathers to his cap which makes him quite unique. He is a four times Guinness Book of World Records Holder in the following subjects :

"Script to Screen" which he achieved by producing and directing a state of art animation film within the shortest time possible by breaking the earlier set record by Canadians. There are many national and international Awards and Recognitions to his credit.

Longest Line of Post Cards which he has done on the occasion of 163 years of Indian Postal Day by 16300 post cards. The event was also connected with a questionnaire about Indian Flag.

Largest Poster Awareness Campaign – This was achieved by designing an awareness campaign on the subject "Beti Bachao – Beti Padhao".

Largest Envelop – Towards tribute to Prime Minister's initiative 'Make in India' – he has created about 4000 sq meter envelop using waste papers.

Attempted by lighting 70000 candles on a 210 kg cake to celebrate the 70th Indian Independence day recorded in World Records India.

Attempted a documentary on Dhamek Stupa of Sarnath dubbing in 17 languages, result is waiting from Guinness World Records.

He is versatile in Gita teaching. The young generation is fond of his Gita teaching and he has changed the life of many young through his continued motivational boost up and teachings.

He has composed and sung Gayatri Mantra in 1000 different tunes.

He has composed and sung Hanuman Chalisa in 108 different tunes.

He has composed and sung hundreds of Sanskrit Bhajans, Patriotic songs, etc.

He has written and directed so many short films and documentaries for awareness campaigns.

He has done voluntary services to UP Police and Kerala Police to spread awareness campaigns on the various issue through videos and photography.

He is on the path of authoring thousands of books on Indian culture, Indian Temples, and the life of extraordinary people.

It is hard to believe that he has produced and directed more than 100 Documentaries on a particular city (Varanasi) which is done by a single person.

He has helped and guided more than 25 boys and girls to achieve world records through various creative and innovative methods.

A multifaceted person who can apply the best of his intellect using the God-given blessings which have been showered upon every human being granting them an immense capacity to learn, experience, and experiment with many things and do wonders in this world of discrimination and disparities.

He is a teacher and a student at the same time who always learns every day and teaches every day. As a master, his weakness was that he never sticks to a particular subject. Perhaps this weakness gives him the strength to master any area which he came across.

Each of his days dawned with learning a new topic and he spend most of his time experimenting and researching it.

He is also a selfless social activist and a motivational speaker.

His life was full of struggle, ups and downs, and failures. But he never gave up and faced all his trials and tribulations full of confidence. Today he is a successful young man with a lot of enthusiasm and rich life experience.

He has sung full Ram Charita Manas 51 hours audio by his own composition. He has also sung the whole Bhagavad-Gita in his own composition with a rhythmic background.

He has also sung "Lokah Samastha Sukhino Bhavantu" in 50 different languages.

Currently working on a detailed and scientific study on Veda, Upanishad, Puranas, Bhagavad Gita, etc.

Currently, he is the Hon' Chancellor of 'Eurasia Digital University'.

Awards

ABOUT THE AUTHOR

Four Times Guinness World Records

Winner of Mahatma Gandhi Vishwa Shanti Puraskar

Mahatma Gandhi Global Peace Ambassador
Kashi Ratna Award

Dr. APJ Abdul Kalam Motivational Person of the Year 2017

Mother Teresa Award

Indira Gandhi Priyadarshini Award

Bharat Vikas Ratna Award

Udyog Ratna Award

Vigyan Prasar Award

Poorvanchal Ratn Samman

Preface

We need to enter into a lot of actions means, we need to do various karmas. Reading a lot of spiritual books and attending motivational classes are not enough to become an expert to balance the mind, but we need to face and chase various adverse situations of life to permanently fix the teachings within us what we learn from scholars, books and motivational classes. Then only the ignorance will remove and get complete wisdom.

This book emphasis on :

1. Selfless Action – Practical Knowledge, applied action.

2. Through achieving wisdom and intelligence - Theory

THEORY AND PRACTICAL OF EVERY ACTION

1. Selfless Action – Practical Knowledge, applied action.

2. Through achieving wisdom and intelligence - Theory

Suppose, there is a swimming competition is going to happen in your school after six months. You want to participate in it, but you don't know swimming. Since you are so desperate to swim and participate in the competition, you have ordered a book online "How to learn swimming". The book has come and you have read the whole book ten times. Now, will you be able to swim in a pool? No. To practically learn swimming you need to get down on the swimming pool and to try hard practice to swim under a trainer. Initially, for a couple of weeks, you will find it very difficult to swim and will get tired off very soon.

But after a month's hard practice regularly, you learned swimming, enjoy it hours in the swimming pool and also qualified to participate in the swimming competition.

So, the destination was: Swimming Competiton (God-realization)

Methods to qualify :

1. Book and Trainer *(wisdom and understanding)*

2. Regular practice in a Swimming Pool *(Action)*

Initially, when we are practicing swimming in the swimming pool we will follow the trainee's instruction and the teachings from the book. But once we are perfectly practiced it, becomes a professional swimmer, we never think about the trainee's instruction or the instruction of the book, because the wisdom and intelligence of swimming automatically embedded within us while doing regular practice of swimming.

For example, just imagine when you were learning driving of bike or car. For a couple of weeks, the car or bike was taking you at its will. Without your switching off the bike, it will automatically stop. Without your knowledge, it will increase or decrease the speed. You will be fully concentrated to maintain the distance, gear changing, applying the brake, etc. and you continued to practice for six months.

But just imagine how you will be driving after six months. Will you be thinking when to change the gear when to apply the brake when to race or not to race the accelerator etc.? No. You will be driving smoothly applying all that what you learned and practiced, but all of it happens automatically without your knowledge.

Can you become a doctor or engineer just by reading the book? No. Practical knowledge is compulsory, and once you are an expert, you don't need to remember always, what you learned and practiced, it will be happening automatically.

One person understands from a book that there is electricity in a wire, but never touched and felt it. But once when was repairing a cable, he touched the open part of it while it was plugged in and electrical shock applied on his body and he was thrown away. Now the knowledge fixed within him permanently.

That's why in life also, we need to enter into a lot of actions means, we need to do various karmas. Reading a lot of spiritual books and attending motivational classes are not enough to become an expert to balance the mind, but you need to face and chase various adverse situations of life to permanently fix the teachings within us what we learn from scholars, books and motivational classes. Then only the ignorance will remove and get complete wisdom.

As explained in the swimming competition above, all of our destinations are only one "God-realization or union with the Supreme". To reach there, we need to do a lot of action (karma) and at the same time, we need to achieve wisdom and intelligence (knowledge of it). We will be given different tasks to chase and face various adverse situations in life. Some will be easy to face and some will be hard to face. But we must face it and to overcome the situation to move forward to the next level. When you face and overcome a situation (action), you achieve wisdom (practical knowledge – permanently fixed understanding).

At the end of the first chapter of this book, I had mentioned that there are two sides to every problem/

situation. Left and Right. Left is the reason for the problem and in right there are multiple options to overcome it. When we overcome it (we achieves wisdom and knowledge of how we did overcome it).

Left Side - Reason - Ignorance (bad karma)

Right Side – multiple options (Practical Knowledge to overcome and removed ignorance). But mostly we stick to the left side thinking that there are problems, problems because of it, problems because of that, problems because of him, problems because of lack of something, etc.

We all know the story of Thomas Alva Edison who invented the bulb. (His story says that he was too stupid to learn anything and he was fired from his first two jobs for being "non-productive")

But he decided to enter into an action.

His aim (destination) was: to invent the bulb

Left Side: Ignorance and problems

Right Side: 1000s of methods to try, by keeping on trying one by one method, finally he reached the destination (invented).

But he is not only just reached the destination by inventing the bulb, but also at the same time, he gained a lot of practical knowledge.

***

An important quote to note :

Somebody has given you a lock to unlock it with any key and offered a highly expensive wonderful gift that will make you rich (Supreme). Condition is, it should not break, you have to find out a perfect key that can unlock It and you are free to try any key. If you are keen to get that expensive gift, you will try to open it with different keys, if you are not serious to have it, then you will give up after a few trials. You have multiple options and you are free to choose whether you want to try again and again or to give up and live in the present lifestyle.

***

Here in life, ignorance is like dirt or dust in our minds. Through continuous action (doing different karmas), we need to clean it perfectly. Even one percent remains, it will disturb. In swimming and driving, if you have even one percent doubt somewhere, you cannot drive or swim smoothly.

Escaping from problems will never make you free from ignorance or make you free from adverse situations. It's like an unsolved question in your examination. You need to solve it to pass it.

***

The desires and attachment on many things will be there even if you live in the forest or Himalayas until you clean your mind completely by chasing and facing the adverse situations in life. If you have achieved "wisdom and intelligence" and if your mind is purified, then you don't need to escape from life. You will find peace even in a crowd and a loud atmosphere. Remember the story of a doctor I had mentioned earlier who attends thousands of patients in a crowd and a noisy atmosphere with a cool mind.

If there are two saints in the Himalayas, and people comes around to meet them to get spiritual teachings. One has more visitors and the other one has fewer visitors. This variation in visitors may generate an ego in one's mind. It means that the saint has still to get complete purification of mind. Enough theory has been practiced, but practical knowledge lacks, that's why mind disbalance happening.

Changing the dress, changing the location, changing the situation, changing the food, etc. won't purify your mind and keep you away from the attachment and desires. Be in the same location or situation, face it, chase it and overcome it then only purification of mind happens through practical knowledge. The mentality of your mind changes from "not possible to possible".

Through continuous practice of chasing and facing, we need to permanently remove the ignorance and to feed the wisdom and knowledge, like an experienced driver drives the car without the tension on how to drive the car when to change the gear, when to apply the brake, etc. The car was smoothly moving but the driver doesn't know, when he changed the gear, when he applied the brake, etc. ***Now the practical knowledge of diriving which is permanently embedded in the mind of the driver drives the car***, not the driver as a person. Earlier you were not aware of a route to reach a destination, but after you traveled the same destination multiple times, you are not worried about the route and now reach the destination without any confusion. The route map is fixed (permanently embedded) in your mind.

Suppose, we have taught good habits to one of our children in their childhood days, but when he shifted to a different city for his further studies, he has forgotten what was taught by the parents and started to enjoy smoking, drinking, etc. with friends, why? Because we taught him in an atmosphere where the parents were not smoking and drinking. But as soon as the location changed, the child gets into that. The teaching he got at home was like swimming learn by book, it was not permanently embedded in the mind.

A person early in the morning sits for meditation to control the mind and to purify it. As you are at the peak of it, the next door, the child of a neighbor started crying loudly. You lost your concentration, raised your anger and said that the child of the neighbor is not allowing me to meditate peacefully.

***

An important quote to note :

Yes, the child won't allow you to meditate peacefully, but you have to practice to meditate peacefully when the child cries. You have to practise meditation again and again in a noisy atmosphere until you reach a level where no mind disturbance or disbalance happens. The state of mind balance (irrespective of situations around you), you have to permanently embed within your mind.

***

A pool looks perfectly clean from the top but when you throw a stone on it, all dirt comes out. It means, still the dirt was there in the river. An outside force when entered into it, the dirt comes up.

Let me recall the story of Buddha...

Once the Buddha was walking through a forest with his disciples and in between on the road, somebody was abusing Buddha very badly. His disciples were so angry but were not responded, because Buddha was walking straight towards the destination silently without even looking to the person. When they reached the destination, the disciples asked Buddha, why he is not reacted or responded to the person who was abused Buddha. Buddha asked his disciples to imagine a situation that somebody on the road is offering you a parcel of junk foods which you have not accepted, then where the parcel will remain? The disciple replied that it will be with him only who was offering it. The disturbance of disciple shows that they have accepted it thats why they are angry with him, but Buddha was not accepted that's why he is silent and cool. The action of that person could not make any change in Buddha's mind because he has achieved and permanently embedded peace of mind in any situation.

***

An important quote to note :

Anger of Buddha's disciples won't come from outside, nobody offered it to them or thrown on them, it was already existed in their mind, which has come out when they reacted to a situation like we throw a stone to a clean water pool

***

You don't need to praise you or condemn you, the mirror will tell you the truth. If you are black, it will show you that you are black, if you are fair, you will look fair in the mirror. Your action and reactions to a situation will show up automatically whether you are selfish or angry. So, clean the mind, not the mirror.

But a mirror is necessary to show you how you look. Whether it is black or fair, no issue, but through a mirror, you will be able to realize the fact. Now you can apply various methods to change from black to fair. If you understood that you are angry and possesses a nature to take revenge, etc. then you should try to clean your mind applying various methods.

***

Acharya Vinobaji narrated a story of a rich person who kept all his expensive pieces of gold jewelry in an iron box to save from thieves. But the value of jewelry and his attachment to it has forced him to change the iron box to the golden box with a gold lock. Earlier it was difficult for the thief to find out where the gold jewelry is, but now, even though, it is safely locked inside the box, the shine of the box itself reveals where it is.

Our habits, attitude, and qualities will reflect in our action.

***

We are born here to perform our duties following the law of karma or the rule of the Supreme, to satisfy the creator or the Supreme. Until the complete mind purification continues, we will suffer and will have more births. When we achieve it, we will be called back by the Supreme to stay with him, that's our ultimate destination. But our perfection in our duties and actions depends on the purity of mind free from attachment, desires, etc.

But what most people do? They behave like the Krishna is authorized them to check the behavior, attitude, quality of lifestyle and actions of others and to react and improve them. They are in a false belief that they are perfect in everything and all others are imperfect and needed purification.

A perfectly purified mind, who has achieved permanent wisdom (gyaan) through practical experience will think like :

Whatever happens, I won't react, whatever happens, I won't cry, what happens, I won't angry, whatever happens, I won't drink, whatever happens, I won't smoke, whatever happens, I won't abuse, whatever happens, I won't condemn anybody, whatever happens, I won't fight with anybody, whatever happens, I won't think negative.

The sun spreads light and energy and which we use it for our various purposes. Sun never worries whether we used it for good purposes or bad purposes. Somebody reading making sweets and somebody making weapos. Whatever, it will just perform its duty by spreading light and distributing energy. *The action (vikarma) is automatically happening because the duty is embedded within it* like the knowledge of driving is embedded within the driver after thorough practice.

***

If one has achieved universal wisdom and it is permanently embedded in his mind with a perfect purification, then whatever a person does will be for the benefit to others only. He does not need to think about what karma to do what should not do. *He may not be doing anything, but the karma happens as the Sun does its action.*

Perfect purification means, immense of goodness and qualities the same as the Supreme. You will be able to do wonders and extraordinary things in the world.

Just imagine, within the shortest time, how Vivekananda reached in the heart of everybody, how Pandit Madan Mohan Malivya alone established one of the greatest universities in the world, how Dr. APJ Abdul Kalam managed to make missiles and became the President of India. They all had to face many adverse situations in life, lack of resources was there, no advanced technology was available at that time, they all had 24 hours like us, they all were taking the same food as we take. Still, they could boom up their talents and capabilities, because of purified perfect mind with immense goodness and qualities within it.

Perfection and purity mean that the mind is filled with ultimate wisdom (gyan) and intelligence (budhi-vivek) which are forcing them to do bigger things. Even a little bit impurity, will disturb the mind and stop from doing bigger things like a damaged apple can damage other apples in the basket.

When we boil the water, the steam (an invisible gas) comes, it looks simple, but if we collect the same steam inside a pressure cooker, then it becomes powerful and can even blast. The same happens with the steam engine of a train.

If the steam is filled with goodness, your action will also be highly powerful and the blast of your goodness will spread around the world and you will live in the heart of billions of people as a great inspiring personality like Dr. APJ Abdul Kalam, Mahatma Gandhi, Swami Vivekananda, etc.

But if the steam is filled with illness, evil thoughts, anger, revenge, etc., then they will be spreading evils or illness to others and will remain as notorious in the heart of the people.

****

Our country Bharat is considered the place where the ancient rishis had spread the wisdom of light around the world, never tried to conquer any country, but others had conquered us. Why one will conquer, to loot the immense wealth and wisdom. No thief will enter an empty house.

When the Coronavirus spread around the world, some countries were blaming a country for its responsibility that they created it. (the real fact is unknown). Even if it is done by a human or a group of humans to disturb and kill the human around the world, just think about the height of cruelty thoughts, which they carry in their minds.

****

In the previous chapter, we have mentioned the importance of maintaining silence. Silence happens from a purified perfect mind. Being in silence doesn't mean that he does nothing, instead, he does more than other people can do. Silence happens from a balanced mental state, by keeping away from our intervening to other's actions, attitudes, attachments and control over physical and material desires.

Just imagine that one person is abusing and the other is maintaining silence without reacting to it. What would happen?

The person who is abusing will create a lot of bad karma, loss of mental peace and creates unnecessary sound vibration in the atmosphere. (bad karma – the action of ill-nature).

The other person being in silence has generated a lot of good karma, achieved mental peace, avoided unnecessary sound vibration in the atmosphere (good karma - inaction). *He has achieved good karma being in silence.<u>Being in silence and by not reacting to anything</u>was the action he did which is called inaction. Did nothing, but happened everything.* Sun does nothing but millions of actions happens in the world 24 hours.

That is why it is rightly said "maunam vidvaanu bhooshanam" – silence is the jewel of wise people.

***

A person who struggled and won will motivate you but the energy won't last in you for long brcause you listened to it but not experienced it. To experience, you have to get into action and sacrifice a lot of things like abuses, condemnation, thirst, hunger, etc.

***

Sins will never touch you if you have achieved the mind balancing stability in every situation. Every problem starts when the mind disturbs and sins also happens from it. But when you understand that everything happens per karma, action and guna dominance in a person, then there is no pain arise in your mind.

<u>Karma Yogam (the state of mind while doing every karma)</u>

Yogam (the state of mind) – those who have achieved a balanced mind, mental stability, sacrificed the me-mine attitude, no attachment, no possessiveness, completely purified mind.

***

Your mind disturbs in many ways, one while you do an action (karma) and 2nd when your friend does an action (karma).

Let's see the following examples :

Example - 1

1. You have attended an exam and failed **(your action)** – your mind is disturbed. *(here, you have failed in your own action, that's why you are disturbed)* – <u>*your feeling of failure/loss is the actual action and the reason,*</u> *which has disturbed your mind – not the exam)*

Example - 2

After one month, you came to know that....

2. Your friend got a government job **(other's action)** - *(by other's action, your mind is again disturbed) – your feeling of jealousy is the actual action and the reason, which has disturbed your mind – not his action of getting the job)*

Example - 3

3. In suspicion, you have checked the wallet of your sister and find a love letter in it - **(your action & other's action** *both are involved - your feeling of suspicion and checking other's privacy is the actual action and the reason, which has disturbed your mind – not her action)*

Since, everywhere, your actions are responsible for disturbing your mind, because of the feeling of failure in the exam, feeling of jealousy and the feeling of suspicion, you itself is responsible for the consequences. Through your actions, you develop sins and virtues, and per the number of sins and virtues, you reap goodness or illness in your life.

In a family, a guest has come. He was the childhood friend of the husband. They welcomed him and forced him to stay there for two days with them and he agreed. The next day evening, the wife did a small complaint to her husband about the friend who is staying there with them. The wife said, he takes alcohol. But the husband didn't know about it and asked her how does she know about it. She said that she has tried to see his room through the keyhole last night and saw that he was drinking something like alcohol.

Just see here.....

In _suspicion_ she tried to check the _privacy_ of the guest and what she has seen is "Something like Alcohol" he is taking and she has fixed it in her mind that she was taking alcohol.

Whether he took alcohol or not, leave it.

Why did you _suspect_, whey did you check somebody's _privacy._

From the next day onwards her behavior has changed, she even doesn't allow his husband to spend a lot of time with him and when the husband returns from his room, she started to suspect her husband also if he has also taken alcohol.

So here, who was the patient and who require the treatment?

***

Gita 5/14 – most important verses with ultimate wisdom

The Supreme (Krishna) hasn't authorized anybody to take ownership of anything or anybody and even not forced, suggested or specified to do this action, that action, etc.

Whatever action (karma) one do, depends on their nature, character, behavior or attitude (per guna dominance within them). That's why whatever goodness or illness happens in one's life depends on the sins or virtues they have created through their actions.

Krishna (The Supreme) sent his own form only and in that form, Krishna's own duty or actions was already embedded (like the Sun). If one follows that, they can see Krishna in them and them in Krishna.

Just imagine your entry into the world.

From nothingness, from an invisible cell in your mother's womb, your body was created, then the form of Krishna (Soul) with the duty and action of him he makes you a complete human body. When you landed on earth, you became the owner of you and the owner of many other beings in the world. You became the owner of the land, you became the owner of your father, mother, son, spouse, properties, business, job, etc.,

But Krishna is not responsible for the ownership of what you have occupied. You have occupied everything and became the owner of it, by your own nature, action, attitude or behavior per whatever guna dominance within you. Krishna never makes you poor or richer.

Krishna has sent you his own form with his own duties and activities to be performed (swadharma) by you. But you forget Krishna (the Supreme – creator) and his duties which you had to perform here.

You lived here like you are the creator, you are the master and you are the owner of everything you occupied.

Since you were not serving the purpose for what you have been given birth, Krishna has to withdraw his form from your body. (if I say calling you back, then the ego of "you and your body includes), so that he can send you in a different location like we send our children from a rural school to an urban school for the higher development of your children.

The moment Krishna calls you back, you losses all of your fake ownership, bondage, and attachment with everything you possess like properties, spouse, children, business, etc. and even your active body (Shiva) becomes a dead body (Shava). All those whom you loved, will hesitate to even touch it.

You lost all that "I am", I am bigger, I did this, I earned this, I owned this, I made this, I am in love with this, I can't live without this, I have everything, I am living for this, etc.

Now, where is that "I am"?

Started from Nothingness (zero – shoonya) and ended in Nothingness (zero – shoonya).

That's why the significance of following Vedic mantra for peace :

"Om Poornam-Adah Poornam-Idam Poornaat Poornam Udachyate Poornasya Poornam-Aadaaya Poornam-Evaavashishyate"

Only the form of Krishna within you had completeness. This completeness has filled the area of nothingness (mother's womb), your completeness happened because of that completeness (Krishna) only, but if that completeness is taken away from your body, you will lose everything (incompleteness) you owned, but that completeness (Krishna) remains even after your body ("I am") becomes nothing.

Started from Nothingness (zero – shoonya) and ended in Nothingness (zero – shoonya).

Your completeness happens when you understand Krishna (The Supreme – The Soul within you), his duties and actions, and you feel, follow, act every action of his which is embedded within you.

When your actions become like the actions of Krishna which are embedded with you, your completeness happens (liberation), you become Krishna. No more birth as human need to take, or even if he takes more births, his actions will be desireless, detached and selfless.

***

Let's understand it from the life of Shri Buddha.

When he achieved completeness, the awareness that he is the owner of nothing, not even his body, (achieved wisdom and intelligence), he has left everything and gone.

It was not necessary to leave for forest leaving everything even his parents, kingdom, wife, children, etc., because every King of a kingdom needed a great scholar (Kulguru) also to rule the kingdom. No doubt, Buddha would be greater than the current scholar they have. Then why did he left everything? *(complete renunciation of action – karma sanyasi).*

If we understand this, we will understand this chapter. The answer is given in Bhagavad Gita 7/3, in thousands and thousands of people who are in search of wisdom and intelligence, one from those thousands, achieves completeness.

Let us try to understand differently....

LEVEL-1

Suppose there are 10 Million People across the globe

*Out of 10 million above, 6 million people possess Tamasik Guna dominance and they are just living and enjoying with less humanitarian activities). Illiterate, living in slums, kills animals, living in backward areas, prefer non-veg food only. – we can name them as **"Ground Class People – like Ground Floor of a Building – Studying in LKG-UKG"***

LEVEL-2

Now left 4 million (5% mind purified people)

Out of the 4 million above, 2 million people posses Rajasik Guna dominance and they are living with more good humanitarian activities + little non-humanitarian activities (because of the mix of Tamasik Guna also). More advanced people than above, service class people, like sweepers, cleaners, prefer non-veg. food etc. – we can name them as **"Lower Class People – like First Floor of a Building - Studying in Class 1 to 5)"**

LEVEL-3

Now left 2 million - (30% mind purified people)

Out of the 2 million above, 1 million people posses Satvik Guna + Rajasik Guna + Tamasik Guna. (Striving to setup life, 10 to 5 working people for food and shelter, lot of relationships, veg. & non-veg. food, small business, and job people, temple going, educated too) we can name them as **"Middle-Class People – like 2nd Floor of a Building – Studying in Class 6 to 10)"**

LEVEL-4

Now left 1 million - (60% mind purified people)

Out of the 1 million above, half million (i.e. 50 Lacs) people possess Satvik Guna only – then they will start doing more selfless services and will find satisfaction in it. Interest to find out who am I, why I am here, who is God....these thoughts will develop. (high-class people, enjoying every lavishness, etc. but later when they over enjoy everything, the excessiveness will convert to think back, because even after every enjoyment they won't find the mental piece or pure permanent satisfaction of mind. Fear of God will start, then they start to turn to think about the reality of humans and God. We can name them as **"Upper-Class People – like 3rd Floor of a Building – Studying in Plus2 + graduation) ".**

LEVEL-5

Now left 50 Lacs - **(90% mind purified people)**

Out of the 50 Lacs people, 40 lacs people possess more purified Satvik Guna – then they will start reading spiritual books and will generate a lot of questions within mind about self-existence, the existence of God, good karma, bad karma, etc., he will be away from full-fledged life enjoyments. He will find peace in reading more spiritual books of great scholars, will do more selfless services, etc. and they will follow a Guru. (we can name them as **"Super-Class People – like 4th Floor of a Building" – Studying in Post Graduation + Ph.D.).**

LEVEL-6 (5th Floor – Last Floor) – Studying in D.Litt

Now left 10 Lacs - **(99% mind purified people)**

Out of the 10 Lacs people, 1 lakh possesses more and more purified Satvik Guna – a lot of selfless karma without expecting anything, all of his actions will be a dedication to supreme, detachment from various desires, simple life, simple food, more and more reading, started achieving wisdom and intelligence, multiple qualities will develop, multiple talents will develop, people will be attracted to him, his words and actions will have some divinity, he feels every one as his brother and sisters, whatever he plans for his son, he will plan for others also. He will understand the Soul and Supreme connection, he will satisfy his soul than for anything else in the world. His attitude will be humble and down-to-earth. He will be comfortable even in a silent place or in a noisy place, stable mental balance, more and more people will interest to connect him, his social connections will increase, people will love to listen to him, he will become like a great counselor, he can wipe out and help more people by cultivating good thoughts and actions. Since, his attitude is more simple, silent and different, he has to face more and more adverse situations. If he is a family person, the family won't afford and adjust to his change. They will try to bring him back to their lifestyle. But he has gone through all that lifestyle and now in the state of detachment. For him now every human is equal. Whatever he will do for his brother, he will do it for others also. He does not possess a "me, mine" attitude. He may have to face various consequences from the family and society, people may misunderstand him, will blame him, will defame him, but he will face it with a smile because he only understands the reason behind it. Unable to explain those are in a false belief that everything they possess, they won't die and everything happens because of them.

Since he now understood the Krishna form within him and his duties and actions (swadharma embedded within him), he is in the process of completeness as Krishna. This awareness makes him intelligent to manage every situation without harming others. Even if people react against him, he *will forget and forgive because of his awareness about the level of people.*

Because of the spiritual development, awareness about self, the achievement of wisdom and intelligence, his power and level of action will expand and he will be automatically doing big things which are not easier for a common man to even think.

Eg : Swami Vivekananda (within the shortest time, he taught a lot to people around the world), Mahatma Gandhi (he still lives in everybody's money purse), Dr. APJ Abdul Kalam (he lives in everybody's heart), Pandit Madan Mohan Malviya (he built one of the world's best university of more than two thousand acres and lives in the heart of millions of students).

These people are called **"KARMA YOGI"** – means **"Qualified Souls"** who understood their Krishna form inside and its duties and actions. He understands the nothingness of his body and completeness of Krishna form. But he lives and performs all of his actions being in a family or being in a society like a saint. Earlier I had mentioned the story of a doctor who was attending thousands of patients comfortably with a smile in a crowded and noisy atmosphere. His quality of mind attracts more and more patients to him. He is a government employee and he will get the same salary as other doctors get in the hospital even if he attends 100 or 1000 patients. In the same hospital, there are more than 200 doctors and every doctor attends a maximum of 100 to 200 patients but there are thousands of patients from various parts of the state want to meet him. The spiritual development and purity of mind have expanded his field of action. He is now not even working for a salary, not working for fame, not working for anything in return, he has realized the Krishna form inside and its duties and action (swadharma) works automatically like a driver drives without thinking how to drive.

Such Level-6 achieved Qualified Souls (Karma Yogi) can be a great Scholar (Guru).

After Level 6 – there is no more level to qualify – there is Nothingness – end of worldly life - approx. 20,000 people will be on that level. From Level – 1 to 6, who has to do many karmas to achieve completeness – no worldly/family karmas to perform – no further study, no examinations).

Those "QUALIFIED SOULS – "KARMA YOGI" – WHOM DOES ALL HIS KARMAS LIKE A SAINT BEING IN A FAMILY OR SOCIETY WITHOUT ANY KIND OF ATTACHMENT, DESIRES later promoted to "KARMA SANYASI".

"KARMA SANYASI" – "QUALIFIED TO RENUNCIATE KARMA" AS HE HAS ACHIEVED KRISHNA COMPLETENESS – THEN HE LEAVES THE FAMILY AND SOCIETY AND CHOOSES SOMEWHERE TO LIGHT THE WORLD LIKE "SUN".

All of the above levels does not happen in one birth. The soul has to take multiple births, experience all worldly pleasures, desires, attachments and to face many adverse situations and to overcome it. Each level will quality from Tamasik to Rajasik and then Rajasik to Satwik and being in Satwik, he will become a **"QUALIFIED SOUL – KARMA YOGI"** and then **"QUALIFIED TO RENUNCIATE KARMA – KARMA SANYASI"**

Buddha had already achieved the 6th level as **"Qualified Soul" – "Karma Yogi"** from his past birth itself that's why it was difficult for him to adjust in his family when he has achieved the level as **"QUALIFIED TO RUNCIATE KARMA" means "KARMA SANYASI"** in his new birth at Kapilavastu.

"Qualified Soul" – "Karma Yogi" will perform his duties as a Saint or a Guru being in a family or society. He will help to develop the other group of people from Level one to five.

"Qualified to renunciate Karma" – "Karma Sanyasi" will become like Sun and he will light the world with wisdom. For him, the whole world and every creature become his family, no relationships, no discrimination, no society *(becomes Krishna itself but being in the body)*.

(KARMA YOGI UNDERSTAND KRISHNA FORM AND HIS DUTIES, BUT KARMA SANYASI COMPLETELY ACHIEVES IT BECOME LIKE KRISHNA)

Buddha was a *"Qualified Soul – Karma Yogi"* but one day while in the family, he achieves completeness, he united with Supreme, which means become a "Karma Sanyasi – Qualified to renunciate Karma – becomes Krishna itself".

For example :

There is a **Chairman***(Karma Sanyasi)* of the Company, the **Managing Director***(Karma Yogi)* works under him, many **Managers***(developed souls)* work under the MD and other staff ***(underdeveloped souls)*** work under a Manager.

(Please recall here the story narrated in the previous chapter about a Boss and his employee who visited Australia, Singapore, etc.)

Level 1 to 5 (Peon to Manager – approx.. 90% people)

(working to get higher-level – promotions – can access up to MD only, no access to Chairman)

Level 6 – Managing Director – (approx.. 9% people)

"Qualified Soul" – "Karma Yogi" (Do everything, but happens nothing)

(working under the Chairman, he has to obey Chairman only. He has to look after him and managers under him.)

Final stage as CHAIRMAN (Boss) – (approx. 1% people).

"Qualified to renounce Karma" (Do nothing happens, everything)

For the Chairman (Boss), his company and all other employees are equal because his company runs because of them). He does nothing, but MD and others do. Chairman *does nothing **"no karma"**, just sitting, but all company works and management happens because of MD and other staff.). This is called **"Qualified to the renunciation of Karma"***

Retirement will be his end of life. No more further post there. Only those people will take birth who has to complete Level 1 to 6 to reach completeness (Chairman - Boss). To reach completeness, all one has to face many life situations through karmas.

Earlier level, by ignorance of body as soul, will do bad karmas, and develop desires and attachment to it. Later he will start achieving wisdom that the body is perishable, nothing registers on the body, without a soul, our body is a dead body and because of this awareness, he will start doing good karmas.

After achieving wisdom and awareness, until we are doing every action selflessly for us, for family and the society connected with us even without any attachment or bondage, we will remain as a ***"Karma Yogi – Qualified Soul"***

In any further birth, when the ***"Karma Yogi – Qualified Soul"*** achieves completeness (same as Krishna Form) he detaches from family, society, etc. His Body and soul become one with the full power of Krishna.

That is why we called Buddha as Krishna's avatar.

Buddha as Siddhartha also passed many births and qualified all levels from Level -1 to 6. He might have started from :

(1) Tamasik Karmas - ignorance

(2) Tamasik & Rajasik Karmas - ignorance, selfish

(3) Rajasik Karmas – attachment, physical & material desires

(4) Rajasik & Satvik Karmas – entering into spirituality

(5) Satvik Karmas – Understanding the Soul as truth, searching for a Guru, a lot of studies, purifying the mind, senses, and Soul.

(6) Understood difference between Body and Soul and the value of Soul than the body. He does all karmas as dedication or submission to the Supreme being an instrument of the Supreme. He understands the power of Soul. He becomes a Guru or a great Scholar. He expands his level and talents. Until his thought was that he is a body, expansion was not possible, because the body cannot be expanded, but Soul can unlimitedly.

Once again, I will try to explain through the following example :

1. CITY COUNCILLORS

▼

2. MAYOR

▼

3. MEMBER OF LOK ASSEMBLY (MLA - MLC)

▼

4. MEMBER OF PARLIAMENT (MP)

▼

5. CHIEF MINISTERS (CM)

▼

6. PRIME MINISTER (PM) "Qualified Soul – Karma Yogi"

Qualified to Rule the whole nation – his reach expanded. But belongs to a particular party.

▼

PRESIDENT "Qualified to renunciate Karma" – "Karma Sanyasi"

Do nothing, happens everything. Qualified to sit and watch whether they rule per constitution whoever may be the party they belong to.

*(It's not easy for a City Councillor to reach the President's Level, he has to face all other phases of politics to reach the level as President. It takes many years and has to face many elections, to chase many issues like a Soul to take many births to achieve the level of **Completeness to become – a***

Chairman – a President – a Karma Sanyasi)

More way to understand **<u>Karma Yogi</u>** *and* **<u>Karma Sanyasi</u>**
using different words of understanding

Karma Yogi – Did everything – Happened nothing

*This means he did some action but felt nothing in his mind to
his credit. (nothing felt or happened to his mind).*

*(He does various actions (karmas) regularly. Since he
dedicates all to Supreme towards his duty, he doesn't take its
credit in his mind. So, his mind says that he did nothing).*

*Eg: He has given money to a poor (he did an act of giving),
but he says "I did my duty of giving money to a poor towards
an instrument of God – all credit goes to God", so he says, I
did nothing". Money is a physical thing, belongs to God, me
as a human is a physical thing, but belongs to God, the poor
person is a physical thing, but belongs to God.* **A thing of
God, by a person of God, given to a person of God,** *so
where "I" exist in it. The action of helping happened because
of the feeling of help generated inside my mind, the feeling is
not my body, feeling of help belongs to the Soul. When the
feeling did the action, it means Soul did the action. So being
a human with a body, I did the act of God, but since the
credit goes to Soul, nothing happened to me.*

From a Company's perspective...

*The company Managing Director (Karma Yogi) can't take
the credit that I did everything for everybody. He did various*

duties for his Chairman only. When he does the duties for the direction of his Chairman for the Chairman, how he can say, I did. The chairman hired you to do his duties, you agreed to it and performing it for him. Suppose, the MD has deposited some funds of the company to the bank. The money belongs to the Chairman and his company, MD did the action of depositing it on behalf of Chairman. Chairman is not yours, the company is not yours, money is not yours. Here actually the Chairman deposited the money through you. So whatever happens through your duty is happening for the Chairman.

Karma Sanyasi – Did nothing – Happens everything

(He does no actions but happens everything like sunrise and sunset. Sun stays in his form every day with his (swadharma) embedded quality within (Krishna Form within). No specific connection with anybody and no credit it takes for its action. But through his power and energy, millions of things (actions) happens on the earth. If we ask the Sun, did you light the moon? Sun will say, no "I didn't". Did you remove dark? I don't know, the embedded duty within me is to light permanent).

If we ask the Chairman of a company, did you appoint a new peon in your company? He will say "I don't know, I didn't". I don't need a peon for me. If any of the managers might have appointed, but I didn't. It happened actually in his company since the Chairman is not involved in it, so he didn't.

I tried to explain **"Qualified Soul – Karma Yogi"** & **"Qualified to renunciate Action" "Karma Sanyasi"** in different ways connecting with many life-related incidents. It took more than years of a continuous reading of Gitaby various authors to understand this chapter.

***

More qualities of a Qualified Yogi :

5/18 – it says, A wisdom achieved Soul equally sees (samadarshi) the divine presence in a scholar, cow, elephant, dog or in a low born outcaste person.

It was easy to mention that wisdom achieved soul sees all creatures equally, then why did it has mentioned scholar, cow, elephant, dog, a low born outcaste person, etc.

Actually, it means that wisdom can be achieved by anybody. We cannot say that a Professor of Physics, Mathematics or even a Professor of Sanskrit as wisdom achieved scholars. They are specialized teachers and they have immense knowledge of that particular subject only. If a physics professor teaches about gravity or Brownian motion, it doesn't mean that we can consider him as Sir Issac Newton or Albert Einstein respectively.

Let's understand it with the example of Jagad Guru Aadi Shankaracharya's story.

He's left his home in the childhood itself in search of a Guru to achieve the truth of self (wisdom). He met many Gurus and was taking teachings from them, but still, he was unaware of the real knowledge and wisdom about self.

(wisdom and intelligence mean the understanding of the difference between the perishable body and permanent soul...)

Once Shankaracharya (Shankar) was in Kashi a low born outcaste person (untouchable) was coming from the opposite side of his route. The disciples asked Shakar to keep off from that person. Shankar also told him to keep off. But the low born outcaste person laughed on Shankar and asked who should keep off? He or his body? He then said that his body is made of earth (perishable and impure) but his inner self is all-pervading hence immovable and inert. The soul is a part of the Supreme (Krishna), pure always, but the mind and senses are impure by such kind of thoughts. "When you are saying to keep off, the soul listens to your voice, not body".

The response of that outcaste person enlightened Shankaracharya and understood the difference between body and soul.

He had already met many Gurus and read a lot of literature, but he has achieved wisdom from a lowborn outcaste person. Shankaracharya fell on his feet for forgiveness and considered him as Guru to realizing him the truth.

2nd example...

Once the King Vikramaditya has given a clue of few words and asked the poets to write a small meaningful poem ending with those words.

The clue word was "GULU GUGGULU GUGGULU".

All poets have confused, how can they write a poem with these words which has no meaning and not the words are even available in the dictionary. The same day in the evening when the poet Kalidasa was sitting on a bank of the river, a money was jumping from one branch to another branch of a Jambul (Jamun - Syzygium cumin) tree to collect the fruit of it. While he was jumping a lot of jambul fruit was falling on the river and the water sounds like "GULU GUGGULU GUGGULU".

Poet Kalidasa immediately wrote down a poem :

Jambu Phalani Pakwani

Patanti vimale jale

Kapi kampita shaakhaabhyaam

Gulu Guggulu Guggulu

When the monkey jumps from one branch to another the matured jambul fruits fall on the silent river and it sounds like Gulu Guggulu Guggulu.

So who has given the wisdom and helped Kalidasa to write the poem with those words? No doubt, the monkey.

So an intelligent scholar finds every creation on earth with equal importance for the existence of the universe. The intelligent scholar will have two things in common as mentioned in the verse 5/18 i.e. Vidhya (wisdom), Vinay (humbleness).

Shankaracharya hasn't achieved the real wisdom (vidya) of difference between Body (ego) & Soul (truth), that's why he was not shown humbleness to that lowborn outcaste person and asked him to keep off. When he achieved wisdom – the real truth, humbleness (Vinay) automatically generated in his mind and he falls on the feet of that person.

Body and mind both saluted him.

There is an ultimate secret about Wisdom (Vidya) & Humbleness (Vinay) in one of the future chapters.

***

Once a person reaches the level of "Qualified Soul" – "Karma Yogi" – his desire from the body, attachment to physical and material desires comes to an end. Since the day he understood that the Soul is imperishable, his thought of fear of birth and death ends. He thinks beyond the level of life of birth and death. (5/19)

He won't be happy to have any kind of physical or material thing and won't be sad if lost something valuable. For him nothing valuable than his Soul. (5/20)

Since he maintains a completely purified balanced mind with no desires and detachment with any kind of physical and material things, he always feels permanent peace of mind. He does only those actions which purify his mind and compliment to the Soul (totally selfless by body and mind) for permanent satisfaction and peace. (5/21).

Desires and attachments have the nature of "rise and set" (come and go). When we get it, we become happy, when we lose it, we get sad. Those who understand the principle of permanent peace won't attract in worldly pleasures (5/22).

Those who understood the truth of the Soul and the Supreme, as early as possible before leaving the body, will find the light of wisdom (enlightenment) within him and it will spread around others and will be qualified to become a Scholar with ultimate heavenly peace and thus leads him to liberation (achieves completeness – same as Krishna). (5/23-24).

Such wisdom achieved scholars, even being in the body can achieve liberation (Krishna Form within) because they are free from all sins, suspicion and doubts and lives for the benefit of every being on earth. Either in this birth or next birth, they can achieve liberation. They are very near to it.

Like the MD of a company can become Chairman at any time, maybe this year or next year. (5/25-26)

5/27 to 29 is the introduction of the next chapter so not explaining here.

***

Shuk janak – brahmarpanam brahma havihi…karma yogi

Always in Samadhi mode, nirvikar

Karma Sanyasi looks lie a machine that runs at high speed but looks as stable. Mahavir, Buddha, etc.

Even to become a *Karma Sanyasi,* we need to qualify *Karma Yogi* first. To qualify for *Karma Yogi*, we need to perform a lot of actions (practice & experience karmas). *Karma Yogi* is like a Guru who can help thousands of ignorant people with his light of wisdom and awaken them to understand the real duties and actions to be performed while living.

A *Karma Yogi* can maintain a family and live in a common society. He doesn't need to leave anything. Only his actions will be different than others. That's why it says becoming a **"Karma Yogi"** is most important than "Karma Sanyasi".

Karma Yogi does Sagun Karmas (completely selfless and detached – visible but not felt in mind and no credit of it as he did because he has did it as a duty to the Supreme)

Karma Sanyasi does Nirgun Karmas (invisible like does nothing) but happens everything.

***

Karma Yogi writes something on a paper which is visible and we can read it. (means we can learn and understand him).

But *Karma Sanyasi* writes something on a paper but it is invisible, many people tried to read it but unable to understand. (But only a *Karma Yogi* can understand).

Just check the currency notes, all are made of paper and look equal in size, but some are of 10 rupee value, some 20, 50, 100, 500, 2000 – value is different. The value of the people is also depending on the wisdom and intelligence they have achieved through selfless karmas.

***

Somebody asked if a person as *Karma Yogi (Qualified Soul)* is living in a family or society where all others are of a different attitude like enjoying every worldly pleasure, extreme desire with physical and material things, attachment and bondage with the relationships, then how he will manage and survive the opposition from others.

He is qualified for the *Karma Yogi* status after facing such many adverse situations already in the past. So ninety-five percent he will survive by non-minding other people's attitude by forgiving them, making them understand and by maintaining silence etc.

If extreme pressure happens he may leave the place like a *Karma Sanyasi* before he is qualifying for that. But still, he will be a *Karma Yogi* only, because he will be thinking about the well being of all people including his family also (but not worrying about it).

There was a teacher of a town school who after his retirement was staying with his son and daughter-in-law. The wife was expired and no other family member was not there. His thinking, attitude and living style was as usual like every human being. He spent all of his earnings to buildup the career of his son, even he had been taken a loan for it which he has repaid very recently only.

After retirement, some thoughts were disturbing his mind as he spent his whole life selfishly. His teaching to the student was not that sincere, it was like fulfilling some formality. Never I had shown any interest to bring up a student or build up the career of a student as I had shown interest for my son.

He was transcending from a selfish person to a "Karma Yogi"

So, he now decided to start a free coaching and motivational class at his home for all kinds of students. He used some money from his provident fund, gratuity, etc., plus he decided to use his monthly pension for the well being of students towards his duty, dedication or submission towards God.

A lot of students started to come, and even their parents were also very happy. Everybody in his district appreciated his action and even the media also covered his selfless social service. He was also doing it very comfortably and satisfactorily which he never felt during his teaching profession when he was doing it for a salary.

Once when his selfless services were at his peak, the attitude of his son and daughter-in-law towards him was changed. They disagreed with his attitude and pressurized him to stop it. His son started to blame him, defame him, condemn him and tried whatever he can do with the support of his wife to stop this free service. They even disturbed the classrooms and fired to some students and parents.

His son wanted all of his father's money of provident fund, gratuity, and his monthly pension too. They were so selfish and they don't want any disturbances at their home.

The teacher whispered and said in his mind that *"a man reaps what he sows"*. He brought up his son and built up his career with a selfish mentality and now all that selfishness his son is reciprocating him back.

Since he understood the selfish mentality of his son, he continued with his services without any regret because all his services were for others (selfless), not for him, not for his son and no "I am" doing attitude and the ego of its credit in his mind. Completely dedicated and sharing his knowledge and his earnings.

Even after his son's objection, the teacher was continuing with his services. The ego, anger, discomfort, etc. of his son has increased and he decided to revenge by harming his father. The next day the teacher met with an accident while he was on his morning walk and one of his legs has got fractured. Since he was hospitalized for a couple of months, his study center was closed. When the teacher was discharged from the hospital and when reached back home, he saw that his coaching center was completely demolished by his son.

He understood the situation, balanced his mind and later decided to leave the place and went to his village which was about a hundred kilometers away from town.

He restarted everything, opened a small school and started teaching the poor students of the village. All villagers were very happy and he successfully lived there till he leaves the body.

Points to note from above :

(1) The teacher was living normally with extreme attachment with his son and he has done everything for his son. His job was also just for salary and for feeding his family. *Selfish action to satisfy his bodily attachment.*

(2) After retirement, he has realized that he has to do some selfless action too to satisfy his soul and the Supreme. *Selfless action by doing something for others expecting nothing in return, not even for the name.* **(Became Karma Yogi – Qualified Soul)**

(3) His selfishly brought up selfish son disagreed with it, disturbed the teacher and he tried to harm his father also to stop his selfless services.

(4) The teacher finally left his home and settled in the village and continued his selfless social work.

(He left his home in town and settle down in a village doesn't mean that he became a *"Karma Sanyasi – Qualified to renunciate Karma"*.

He is still a *"Karma Yogi"* – only because of the extreme disturbances, blaming, harming, condemnation, he just changed the location so that he can continue his service with peace of mind.

He will continue as a *"Karma Yogi"* for a few more births and later he will automatically achieve completeness and become a *"Karma Sanyasi"*.

***

Arjuna is not a *Karma Yogi* or a *Karma Sanyasi*. He is still in his developing stage like common ignorant people. Krishna is just advising Arjuna who is doing his graduation that PG, PhD, and D.Litt are also there which he can accomplish one by one by scoring high in all the examinations. Most important is to achieve a PhD degree *(Karma Yogi)*, don't try for D.Litt *(Karma Sanyasi)* because it can't be achieved without a Phd and later when you become more and more expert with further research still being in your PhD career, D.Litt will automatically be given or happen.

The word "sanyasi" in Gita is referred to explain the qualities of ***"Karma Sanyasi"*** but most people think that if somebody follows the teachings of Gita or getting the wisdom of Gita will change their mind and they will become a sanyasi. Changing an orange dress code doesn't mean that he became a sanyasi.

English Text of Sanskrit Slokhas of Chapter-5 for Quick Reference

1

arjuna uvācha
sannyāsaṁ karmaṇāṁ kṛiṣhṇa punar yogaṁ cha śhansasi
yach chhreya etayor ekaṁ tan me brūhi su-niśhchitam

2

śhrī bhagavān uvācha
sannyāsaḥ karma-yogaśh cha niḥśhreyasa-karāvubhau
tayos tu karma-sannyāsāt karma-yogo viśhiṣhyate

3

jñeyaḥ sa nitya-sannyāsī yo na dveṣhṭi na kāṅkṣhati
nirdvandvo hi mahā-bāho sukhaṁ bandhāt pramuchyate

4

sānkhya-yogau pṛithag bālāḥ pravadanti na paṇḍitāḥ
ekamapyāsthitaḥ samyag ubhayor vindate phalam

5

yat sānkhyaiḥ prāpyate sthānaṁ tad yogair api gamyate
ekaṁ sānkhyaṁ cha yogaṁ cha yaḥ paśhyati sa paśhyati

6

sannyāsas tu mahā-bāho duḥkham āptum ayogataḥ
yoga-yukto munir brahma na chireṇādhigachchhati

7

yoga-yukto viśhuddhātmā vijitātmā jitendriyaḥ
sarva-bhūtātma-bhūtātmā kurvann api na lipyate

8, 9

naiva kiñchit karomīti yukto manyeta tattva-vit
paśhyañ śhṛiṇvan spṛiśhañjighrann aśhnangachchhan
svapañśhvasan
pralapan visṛijan gṛihṇann unmiṣhan nimiṣhann api
indriyāṇīndriyārtheṣhu vartanta iti dhārayan

10

brahmaṇyādhāya karmāṇi saṅgaṁ tyaktvā karoti yaḥ
lipyate na sa pāpena padma-patram ivāmbhasā

11

kāyena manasā buddhyā kevalair indriyair api
yoginaḥ karma kurvanti saṅgaṁ tyaktvātma-śhuddhaye

12

yuktaḥ karma-phalaṁ tyaktvā śhāntim āpnoti naiṣhṭhikīm
ayuktaḥ kāma-kāreṇa phale sakto nibadhyate

13

sarva-karmāṇi manasā sannyasyāste sukhaṁ vaśhī
nava-dvāre pure dehī naiva kurvan na kārayan

14

na kartṛitvaṁ na karmāṇi lokasya sṛijati prabhuḥ
na karma-phala-saṅyogaṁ svabhāvas tu pravartate

15

nādatte kasyachit pāpaṁ na chaiva sukṛitaṁ vibhuḥ
ajñānenāvṛitaṁ jñānaṁ tena muhyanti jantavaḥ

16

jñānena tu tad ajñānaṁ yeṣhāṁ nāśhitam ātmanaḥ
teṣhām āditya-vaj jñānaṁ prakāśhayati tat param

17

tad-buddhayas tad-ātmānas tan-niṣhṭhās tat-parāyaṇāḥ
gachchhantyapunar-āvṛittiṁ jñāna-nirdhūta-kalmaṣhāḥ

18

vidyā-vinaya-sampanne brāhmaṇe gavi hastini
śhuni chaiva śhva-pāke cha paṇḍitāḥ sama-darśhinaḥ

19

ihaiva tair jitaḥ sargo yeṣhāṁ sāmye sthitaṁ manaḥ
nirdoṣham hi samaṁ brahma tasmād brahmaṇi te sthitāḥ

20

na prahṛiṣhyet priyaṁ prāpya nodvijet prāpya chāpriyam
sthira-buddhir asammūḍho brahma-vid brahmaṇi sthitaḥ

21

bāhya-sparśheṣhvasaktātmā vindatyātmani yat sukham
sa brahma-yoga-yuktātmā sukham akṣhayam aśhnute

22

ye hi sansparśha-jā bhogā duḥkha-yonaya eva te
ādyantavantaḥ kaunteya na teṣhu ramate budhaḥ

23

śhaknotīhaiva yaḥ soḍhuṁ prāk śharīra-vimokṣhaṇāt
kāma-krodhodbhavaṁ vegaṁ sa yuktaḥ sa sukhī naraḥ

24

yo 'ntaḥ-sukho 'ntar-ārāmas tathāntar-jyotir eva yaḥ
sa yogī brahma-nirvāṇaṁ brahma-bhūto 'dhigachchhati

25

labhante brahma-nirvāṇam ṛishayaḥ kṣhīṇa-kalmaṣhāḥ
chhinna-dvaidhā yatātmānaḥ sarva-bhūta-hite ratāḥ

26

*kāma-krodha-viyuktānāṁ yatīnāṁ yata-chetasām
abhito brahma-nirvāṇam vartate viditātmanām*

27, 28

*sparśhān kritvā bahir bāhyānśh chakṣhuśh chaivāntare
bhruvoḥ
prāṇāpānau samau kritvā nāsābhyantara-chāriṇau
yatendriya-mano-buddhir munir mokṣha-parāyaṇaḥ
vigatechchhā-bhaya-krodho yaḥ sadā mukta eva saḥ*

29

*bhoktāraṁ yajña-tapasāṁ sarva-loka-maheśhvaram
suhṛidaṁ sarva-bhūtānāṁ jñātvā māṁ śhāntim ṛichchhati*

Contact

9839093003

myrichindia@gmail.com

facebook.com/drjagadeeshpillaiofficial

youtube.com/drjagadeeshpillai

www.ingramcontent.com/pod-product-compliance
Lightning Source LLC
Chambersburg PA
CBHW031331130726
47988CB00007B/3083